Longing to Belong

A man's search for peace and for home

Valerie M. Warkentin

Dedication

I dedicate this book to my friend who is the real 'Curtis', for sharing his life and his story with our family, in the hopes that his life can positively influence others.

Preface

This is a fictional story based on a real person.

My hope in writing this story is that readers will gain insight into the thoughts, feelings and background of a person who ended up in prison for many years. I also want to help prevent readers from making similar mistakes as 'Curtis' did.

Another desire that I have is that my readers will observe what the main character found that brought him healing in his life and that this will be applied in their lives.

To any readers discouraged with life, may you find hope for better days ahead.

Feel free to contact me with your questions/comments at pain33heart@gmail.com

Chapter 1

Curtis strode resolutely to the apartment where his twenty-eight year old daughter Lindsey lived with her boyfriend. As he walked by the rows of apartments, he tried to muster up courage, despite his daughter's recent withdrawal from him.

When Lindsey's mother had died seven months ago, Lindsey had called and begged him to move across Canada from Lavender, British Columbia, to Ottawa, Ontario to be with her. He had wanted to but he hadn't been ready, partially because he had no money but mostly because he was ashamed.Throughout his daughter's growing up years, Curtis had been in prison. He had spent many despairing nights thinking of her and wishing he could be the one to parent her. He wanted to repair the damage he must have caused her and longed to connect with her now.

They had talked on the phone occasionally over the years and once he was released from prison, he had come to see her. It hadn't gone well. One time when they met, she was smoking pot and he had knocked the joint out of her hand because he didn't want her to follow the path he had taken with drugs. She had yelled at him and said he had no right to tell her what to do. They were two hurting people, not knowing where to begin.

Curtis continued on his fateful walk, his lean frame pushing against the wind and cold of Ontario's November. Luckily he had been given some snow boots from the Mission when he arrived. Some snow had started to accumulate as winter approached.

Curtis was six feet tall with a shaved head, exposing many tattoos. He had tattoos all over his head, on his chest and up both arms. Some tattoos were there to communicate to others his toughness and some were a reminder to him of his desire to follow God. He liked to be super clean and dress well despite the fact that he often discarded his belongings when heading to a new location. Since generous agencies like The Salvation

Army and The Mission abounded, he was always sure to get whatever he needed at the time.

Curtis had recently come back to Ottawa to stay for awhile and to work on his relationship with his daughter. Lindsey had picked him up from the Greyhound bus station in late August after he had spent three days and nights of travel, anticipating their reunion. She reminded him of his mother with her hefty frame and her tough attitude. Their connection was positive at first although they were both hesitant.

Lindsey had brought Curtis to her apartment where he met her boyfriend Alejandro. Curtis was good at reading people and could quickly tell that Alejandro was not too keen on having him in their place. Understandably, he was protective of Lindsey. Alejandro was latino with a slender but strong build.

Curtis was invited to stay at their apartment for one night, sleeping on the couch. As he lay there not able to sleep, Curtis thought about his relationship with his daughter. He had conflicting feelings and thoughts racing through his mind. How could he possibly have a normal relationship with her now? She was basically a stranger. Even though she looked like family, he had only known her as a baby and a toddler.

Those few connections that they had shared in the past eight years since he was out of prison had been brief and certainly not enough time to know someone. He longed to know who she was and what her thoughts were. He wanted to be a father to her, to protect her and guide her. Perhaps he had missed his chance. It seemed so. Here she was, a young adult, living with her boyfriend and having a full time job. Who was he that she would even want him in her life? He was an ex-convict and a drug addict. Yet he was also a man with a tender heart loved his daughter and wanted a relationship with her.

The next day when Lindsey left for work, Curtis went to spent time with his brothers and then went to stay at a shelter temporarily. Several days later, Curtis met up with Lindsey for supper at McDonalds.

"Dad," Lindsey hesitantly began, "I really need you to promise not to hang out with your brother Anthony and drink with him. He is an alcoholic. I also won't be able to handle it if you do drugs. It would hurt too much since Mom just died of a drug overdose."

"Um, sure, no alcohol or drugs, but I will see my brother Anthony. He's part of the reason I came here. You are the main reason but he is my brother. This also goes for my other brother Paul. I can't promise I won't take the occasional pot, but I won't do speed."

Curtis had thought that had satisfied her but after that conversation, Lindsey became cool and aloof and didn't want to see him anymore. Well apparently, Lindsey had learned that he was drinking with his brother when he said he wouldn't. What was the big deal? Curtis had drank a couple of beers with a brother he hadn't been with for about thirty years. That's what Anthony does - he drinks. Drinking wasn't Curtis's issue anyway.

When he had sat close to her on the couch that first night and put his arm around her, he thought he had been doing the right thing. He had seen his friend Troy's affection with his daughter Willow. Another friend, Ken, hugged his daughters. Yet somehow Lindsey had reacted to that. What did she want from him anyway? It was so confusing.

So he had backed off and waited for the phone call that never came. Then he had called her but there was no answer. After three months of hoping, Curtis was tired of it. He had moved to Ottawa for her. He had always regretted his life and how he had been cut off from her. It was his greatest anguish. she had wanted him and he had come. But now somehow she was done with him.

Now he was going to try one more time. His heart beat faster as he approached her twenty-storey brick apartment building. Reaching the main door of the apartment, Curtis took a deep breath and rang her number. Alejandro answered and came down to the apartment lobby, opening the door a crack. He wasn't smiling and stated flatly, "Lindsey doesn't want to talk with you anymore. Leave now."

Curtis was stunned and disappointed. He had expected something like this but he had hoped for more. "Are you sure?"

Alejandro was adamant, "Go, or I will call the police!" He held his phone in his hand as a threat.

There was no explanation and seemingly no likelihood of future contact. Curtis turned and walked slowly away, almost stumbling as his hope slithered out of him. Then anger rose up and he strode away without a backwards glance. He kicked a garbage can over in his frustration and punched a flower pot at another apartment building, sending the flowers and dirt flying. So much rejection and judgement had come towards him from family members and society. Now his own daughter was turning him away too. Pain moved in his heart again and twisted in his soul. He ran, blinking tears away and not knowing where to go or what to do.

Chapter 2

Lindsey slowly slid across the queen-sized bed to peek out her bedroom window from the third floor of her apartment. Her boyfriend was talking to the man at the door, turning him away because she had asked him to. The man slowly turned and walked away, downcast, slow steps, then walking in an angry manner without a look backward. Her father. The one she hated yet had longed for. The one she had asked to move across the country to be with her. The one she refused to see. Her emotions were a mess! She dropped to the floor and wept.

How dare he drink with his brother when he said he wouldn't! She hated those Stradmores! Drug addicts and convicts! She had hoped her father had changed. Maybe he hadn't after all. She didn't want another drug addict for a parent. Her mom, his ex, had just died of a drug overdose seven months previously. Lindsey had been the one to find her. Years of hoping for a mom who would love her enough to stay clean had ended like that. Lindsey just couldn't try to love another parent and watch him destroy himself. She lit a cigarette and inhaled.

Part of her was happy because she felt successful. Lindsey had grown up in foster care, mostly with one family and they were good to her. She had been cared for and protected. After graduating from high school, Lindsey trained as a hairdresser and had a steady job since age twenty. Alejandro, her live-in boyfriend, loved her and was faithful to her. They'd been together five years now.

Yet this other part of her was there too. Her origins and her parents. She didn't even want to think of the mess that both of them had made of their lives, yet her mind often took her back there.

Lindsey's foster parents, Bob and Cindy, had explained her first few years of life. She was three years old when she came to them. She had been removed from her mom Jill's care because Jill was a drug addict and the neighbours had reported their concerns for Lindsey. Bob and Cindy didn't have any children of their own and they were delighted to take her in. Although they had never formally adopted her, they treated her as their own and she had grown up with their love and their supportive extended family and many friends.

Her childhood had been positive yet she had still longed for a life with her natural parents. She had no memory of them but Cindy had told her about how her dad had been the main caregiver for her the first eighteen months of her life until he went to prison. Her mom had loved to take her to parks and push her on the swings. Then drugs and violence had taken over in her mom's life and Lindsey had gone into foster care.

Lindsey didn't meet her birth mom Jill until she was ten. Lindsey felt awkward but she was drawn to her mom and saw that she had Jill's blue eyes and strong personality. Mom was nervous and skinny. Something about her scared Lindsey and she felt confused. Jill was allowed monthly visits but only with Bob and Cindy there. Lindsey knew that her Jill loved her desperately but apparently she loved her drugs more. There was no going back to her. The courts had decided that when she was four.

When Lindsey was eighteen, she decided that she wanted to spend more time with her mom and get to know her more. Jill was willing to do this and they would meet often. But there were many disappointing moments when Jill did not show up as promised or she would come to their appointed meeting place high on drugs. Who was the person underneath all this addiction?

Lindsey tried to help. She talked with Jill about treatment centres but Jill didn't want to go. For years Jill had lived on the streets.

Often on her way to work on the bus, Lindsey had seen her mom swaggering down the street or dumpster diving. It was pathetic. Lindsey wished that her mom could have a little apartment and get cleaned up but it seemed hopeless. Maybe they could even share a place? Bob and Cindy strongly discouraged that although they did empathize with Lindsey's care for her mom.

One day, Lindsey noticed a For Rent sign on an old apartment building in the downtown area. The building didn't look great but it might be cheap, something that her mom could afford. There was a small bachelor suite available and she knew that her mom could pay for it with her income assistance cheque if she could convince her worker that she was going to be living somewhere besides the street. It was simply furnished which was also a big help. Lindsey decided to take a risk.

"I'd like the place for my mom," she told the landlord. "She will be living here but I will make sure that the rent is paid and that she keeps the place clean."

The landlord was happy to get the suite rented out and signed the intent to rent form. Lindsey looked for her mom in the usual hang out places and told her the good news. Jill was reluctant but relieved at the same time and agreed to look at the place.

The next day Jill moved in. Lindsey went to the local thrift shop and picked up a few items that the suite was missing. Lindsey gave her mom a big hug and told her that she would see her the next day.

January 6, 2014 was to be the saddest day of Lindsey's life so far. Thankfully Alejandro had decided to come with her to see Jill and her new home. Lindsey knocked on the door with no response. Since Lindsey had a key, she opened the door to see if Jill was there.

Immediately her heart leapt as her mom was lying on the floor, completely still. Screaming for Alejandro to call 911, Lindsey desperately tried shaking her mom awake, hoping to find a heartbeat and feel a breath but there was nothing.

Within two minutes, the police and ambulance attendants filled the room. They took control over the situation, checking out Jill. It was too late. Jill was growing cold and had probably died several hours earlier.

Lindsey lay on her mom, screaming and crying. "Mom, come back! Mom! Mom!"

Gently but firmly, Alejandro wrapped his arms around Lindsey and pulled her up. "Let's go. They are taking care of her body."

Lindsey was in shock and grief. She felt numb and she didn't know what to do. She nestled into Alejandro's arms. He spoke with the paramedics and they all headed to the hospital.

Everything was a blur for Lindsey. Testing confirmed a heroin drug overdose. There was no good-bye note. There was nothing. It was over. Lindsey's heart was broken. She had tried and she had failed. Life seemed to seep out of her as well.

Jill had no friends or other family members. A memorial was held in the hospital chapel with some words spoken that Lindsey could not focus on. Alejandro, Bob and Cindy were with her there and the chaplain gave her the urn with her mom's ashes.

Lindsey could not define her emotions. There was a deadness. A loss of hope left despair and sadness in its place. As they exited the hospital, rage stormed up and erupted out of her body. She lifted up the urn and smashed it down on the ground as hard as she could, hoping it would break into a thousand pieces. It didn't but she couldn't look at it again. Alejandro helped her into the car and she watched her foster parents pick up the urn and take it with them. Lindsey jolted away from her thoughts and back to the present as Alejandro entered the room and spoke to her.

"Hey. I got rid of your old man. Let's move on with life. Don't let him get to you. You tried."

Lindsey nodded but her emotions still felt conflicted. Struggling with her thoughts, she let Alejandro pull her up in his strong arms and held hands with him as they walked into the kitchen to prepare a thai chicken stir-fry for supper.

Chapter 3

Oh, this miserable life. And there was no escaping it. Curtis had tried. Oh, he had tried, with drugs to numb his mind and numerous suicide attempts. But here he was, still alive, angry and upset about his daughter's rejection of him.

Since he had arrived in Ottawa mid-August, he had spent his nights at The Mission or under a bush in a park. Now that his disability money had come through and the weather had cooled, he had moved into an old run-down rooming house. At least he was alone in his room at night but the building was full of people on drugs and he had to share a bathroom with other residents down the hall. He didn't want to associate with them and was afraid of the pull of drugs since he knew drugs would help him to forget his emotional pain. It did not feel like a home where he felt safe, loved and that he belonged.

As he lay on his creaky single bed, early memories pushed their way into his mind again, like unwelcome but persistent intruders. There was no escape from the truth of his past. This was his life. His grandmother, who had lived with the family when he was growing up, had locked him up in his bedroom multiple times as a punishment. His siblings called him stupid. Their house had been a mess with cat poop, dog hair, garbage and dirty laundry strewn everywhere. Now he was a clean freak. He had frequent showers to comfort him but also to try to wash off the filth that he couldn't seem to erase from his body. He kept his space spotless and orderly. How had he survived the disorder and chaos of his childhood and why had he? His life did not make sense to him. He did not want it but he could not escape it.

Curtis was the second youngest in a series of five children. His brothers were Patrick, Paul and Anthony. His sister Donna was the last born. They had lived in a small townhouse in a housing complex. Police were at their house frequently, breaking up fights between his mom and grandma, between his mom and dad, and later busting the boys for drugs.

He had conflicting feelings about his mom. She was not a typical mom who provided well for her children. There were some positive memories, such as when she made an abundance of pies and each of the five kids could have one to themselves. Curtis's favourite was lemon. Biting into a piece of lemon pie now brought back those rare moments of being cared for and feeling safe.

Those favourite foods and special memories were not many. Often there was no food or very little that Curtis and his siblings had to find and prepare for themselves. Curtis's mom weighed about four hundred pounds and so was not very mobile. She had diabetes which eventually claimed her life at age sixty-three. Grandma and Mom would have vicious verbal and physical fights. Curtis shivered, remembering the many beatings given to him by his grandmother.

Curtis's dad was the father of all five siblings, yet had never lived in their home as far as Curtis could remember. Curtis had spent some weekends at his dad's cabin in the woods but it was a very uncomfortable place for him because his father and his father's friends were gang members. There was a lot of shouting and fighting and drugs going on. These men were Curtis's role models for manhood. They were mean, they were feared and they had all the money they wanted from their drug deals. Part of Curtis wanted to be with his dad and to be like him, but mostly he felt repulsed.

Chapter 4

Home was crazy and school turned out to be another nightmare. Most of the teachers were afraid of Curtis because he was so aggressive and no one could control him. He was always put in special classes but very little learning took place because he couldn't focus and he continually acted out his anger.

At age eleven, Curtis mustered up courage to go and talk with a school counsellor. "I need out of my home. It's making me crazy. Mom and Grandmother are always fighting. It's a mess. I'm scared of Dad and his drug buddies. Please help me."

The counsellor took off his glasses and looked at Curtis dismissively.

"Foster homes are hard to find. There is no use bothering the social workers with your concerns. They are only able to help kids with more serious problems of abuse or neglect. Now go back to class and focus on your work!"

Curtis abruptly left and slammed the door behind him. Intense anger moved its way up his body and erupted through every cell. *Go back to class?! I don't think so!* Curtis ran out of the school before anyone could block him and didn't stop until he could run no more.

Since foster care didn't seem to be an option and the school counsellor wasn't in the mood to listen or help, part of Curtis despaired. He was sick of his living environment and so he decided to check out the streets.

He was only eleven but he didn't want to go back to school and he didn't want to return home either. The first night away from home, he slept under a bush at a local park. The next day he managed to steal a lady's purse from a bench when she wasn't looking. He slipped the cash into his pocket and trashed the purse. Retreating to a bathroom in the local shopping mall, he discovered he had scored well. He counted out five hundred dollars cash. He decided to leave Ottawa before his family and the school authorities began to search for him. He went to the Greyhound bus station and when the ticket master asked him where he was going, he read the name Calgary on a sign and replied, "Calgary please."

Then he was off on his adventure, heading west. From age eleven to nineteen, he lived in Calgary, Edmonton,Vancouver and other cities in between. Getting away from Ottawa had been easy, but now life was basic survival. There were some shelters he stayed in but he also slept on the streets, under bridges and in the stairwells of hotels. He was physically beaten multiple times and experimented with drugs, becoming a crack cocaine addict by age fourteen. He was able to get meals and basic necessities from the Salvation Army shelter and other outreach centres but also stole money and sold drugs. The worst part of his days on the streets was being a male escort in order to pay off his drug loans. Gradually it seemed that he was losing himself.

By age nineteen, he decided to return to his home city of Ottawa, hoping that life had improved there. His family took him back in for awhile but he drifted in and out of home and the streets. He daily wondered where he truly belonged or if there was such a place anywhere.

Chapter 5

Curtis woke up sweating, trying to reorientate himself. He sat up. Where was he? He sank back down in his bed, relieved. Of course, he was in his rented room in the dilapidated rooming house in Ottawa where he'd lived for almost four months. Dreams always attacked him in the night - dreams of violence and sex gone terribly wrong. The worst thing about these dreams was that parts of them were true. Every morning he had to calm himself, ground himself in his new reality and make it through another day.

There was no escaping his past. There was no way he was going to do hard drugs again but pot was okay. It was essential. It was the one thing that could relax him and it was almost legal besides.

Curtis dragged himself out of bed, had a quick shower and went to grab his mail. He was excited to see that his monthly disability cheque had arrived. Ripping open the envelope, Curtis was shocked to see that the cheque was two hundred dollars short! What was that about? He had to know right away!

Curtis hopped on his bike and tore off to the ministry office, swearing as he went. He took the time to lock up his bike as he didn't want it stolen. He stormed into the building and up to the first wicket. Luckily, there was no line-up, which was unusual.

Leaning heavily on the counter, with his hoodie over his head and eyes glaring, Curtis bluntly spoke his mind, "So, what's up with my cheque? Why is there two hundred dollars less than there should be?"

Mr. Tom Jones was standing behind the counter. He had stood there for about thirty years. He was short, balding, wore rounded glasses and was unnerved by this bravado.

"Well, I'm not going to tell you why and neither is anyone else when you talk like that!"

Instantly, Curtis jumped the counter and smashed against the plexiglass that was separating them. The glass was too strong to break, but Curtis's outburst caused a quick reaction. Curtis was immediately surrounded by the burly security guard and two other men who showed up from behind the counter. They quickly escorted him outside while Curtis swore and called out about 'his rights'.

Curtis unlocked his bike and raced away, driving like a crazy man along the Rideau Canal for about an hour before he turned his bike around and headed home. Finally his heartbeat slowed down. He was lucky to not have been arrested for his outburst although now he would no longer be able to enter that building. He thought to himself, *That stupid government! I'll show them! They can't mess with me and screw up my life and expect that I will take that!!*

Curtis got to his building, hopped off his bike and brought it into his room. He collapsed on his bed, fuming. He got up, paced around, had some coffee, took a long hot shower, cooked and ate some eggs. He played loud music, watched television and stayed alone for about three days until he could feel that he had calmed down again and was more rational.

He called his brother Paul and asked if his girlfriend Joanne could call and enquire about his cheque. Later she called back and explained that it was a one time two hundred dollar cut because of a shift in the time that the cheque came out. It was lousy but there was nothing to be done about it.

A few days later, Curtis was over at Paul's place for dinner when the phone rang. It was his friend Sophie from British Columbia. Curtis told her about the incident at the office as she listened. He began to get very worked up, talking about how the government had ruined his life.

"The government allowed a woman with a grade four education to raise five kids." Curtis blurted out.

"My dad continually beat up my mom and had to leave the house. The counsellor at school wouldn't contact a social worker to remove me from the house even though I begged. I got into trouble on the streets with petty crime and with drugs at a young age.

"Why didn't anyone help me so that I didn't have to live the life I lived and am living? Why didn't anyone rescue me? I know I'm responsible for taking drugs and for doing that awful thing when I was drunk and high on drugs but then the government locked me up for twenty years! How was that helpful? I had to be violent to protect myself. I hate the government! If they think I'm going to take any more abuse, they can think again!! I have the right to ask a reasonable question and get a reasonable answer and not be treated like a scumbag!

Who does that little weasel of a man think he is anyways, talking with Curtis Stradmore like that? I deserved to be treated with respect, the same as everyone else!!!!!"

Sophie didn't try to reason with him because she knew from past experience that Curtis was not in the frame of mind for advice. She sympathized with his frustration and encouraged him to let it go.

After the call, Curtis felt restless. He was so tired of living in Ottawa waiting for life to improve. He just wanted to leave and return to **British Columbia**, to be with his friends who loved him and didn't judge him for his past. Curtis realized that he was gradually getting more out of control. This had happened many times in the past and he didn't like where it was going. There were too many slips of taking speed and more angry outbursts. When he got his next cheque, he was taking the bus out of here and going back to **British Columbia**

Christmas was fast approaching. Curtis mulled it over and decided to stay in Ottawa to spend it with his brothers. Curtis and his brother Anthony got together with Paul and Joanne in their little apartment, had a turkey dinner and watched football. Although there wasn't deep conversation, Curtis enjoyed being with his brothers. Anguish came to his heart as he thought of his daughter, but he forced himself to think about anything but her.

Chapter 6

Several weeks passed and one Sunday morning Curtis decided to go to church. At eleven a.m., Curtis sat at the back of the church shivering. He had taken a bus from his place and then walked twenty minutes in the cold and snowy January day. But he also shivered for other reasons that he couldn't name. Perhaps it was expectancy. He felt that God had something special for him today. What it was, he had no idea. But he had woken up with a strong beckoning to go to church.

He did come here often, but not every week. This was the church of his childhood: St Andrew's Catholic church. The old building was familiar to him and comforting. Built in 1827, it was the third oldest church building in Ottawa. Sometimes he had come here with his mom when he was really young, but until recently he hadn't been back to this church since he was ten. That was the age when he started to leave his family and to leave the God he had never understood : the God who was distant and didn't seem to have answers to his questions.

The congregation stood as the priest came in, lighting candles. Out of the corner of his eye, Curtis noticed a native man come late into the service and sit down on the same pew, a couple of feet away. He was about Curtis's age, with a long jagged scar on his left cheek. He was stocky and rugged. Somehow Curtis felt intrigued by him.

The service continued and went through its familiar routines. The priest gave his message as Curtis's mind wandered off. Then his mind snapped back to the present when he heard the priest say, "God keeps His promises".

Promises : that was something Daniel, his mentor, had drilled into him. God cannot lie. His word is true. If He promises something, He will deliver. This is a hope and a truth to hang on to. Curtis recalled a promise Daniel had believed for him. It seemed too good to be true. This promise was for him, after he had thought his life was ruined for good and that all life was for now was to get through each day and hope for an early death.

Curtis allowed his mind to ponder the promise from Romans 8:28, "And we know that in all things, God works for the good of those who love him…" (NIV). Daniel had said that God could take the negative things in Curtis's life and use them for a positive future. Sometimes Curtis dared to believe this could be true.

Then the service was over. People were getting up and moving out of their pew and down the aisles. Curtis rose to leave as well when a low male voice startled him. It was the native man he had noticed earlier.

Chapter 7

"Hey - got a moment? My name is Nathan." Nathan extended his hand and Curtis shook it.

"Um, this may sound crazy," Nathan floundered, "I feel God told me to meet you here. Do you have time for lunch?"

Curtis gulped. Of course he had time for lunch. There was nothing better to do. Nothing really to do at all. A free lunch was always a good plan.

"Well, I guess. But I don't have any money."

"No problem." Nathan replied, "It's on me."

Curtis grinned to himself as he followed Nathan out the door. Another person scammed. Now he'd probably get a ride in a warm snazzy car. But no, Nathan was heading across the street to Burger King. So much for a high class dinner or all you can eat buffet. But how can a person complain with a free meal?

Curtis studied Nathan as he followed him into the restaurant. Nathan was self-assured and tough, not someone to mess with. It's not that Curtis wanted to butt heads with Nathan but after his years of vigilance in protecting himself, Curtis naturally studied people, watching for warning signs or what their weak points might be.

"What do you want to eat?" Nathan's question cut into Curtis's reverie.

"Oh, a bacon burger, fries and coffee, double sugar. Thanks."

"Sure." said Nathan, "grab a table, would you?"

The place was crowded but Curtis spotted an open table near a window. A few minutes later Nathan came with their meals and sat down.

"Curtis, it's a bit crazy that you would join a complete stranger for a meal."

Curtis shrugged and Nathan continued as he unwrapped his burger. "I woke up this morning and God spoke to me right away. *Go and find a man, about six feet tall, slim, wearing glasses and with tattoos on his arms, neck and head.*

I was walking down the street, asking God where to find this man. I felt Him say that he was inside the Catholic church. When I sat on the bench, I was pretty sure that it was you. I've got to ask you, do you have tattoos on your arms and your head?"

Curtis removed his coat and rolled up his sleeves. Definitely tattoos. He slipped off his toque. Yes, there were tattoos all over Curtis's shaved head. Nathan was a little stunned.

"You are the man. That's for sure."

Curtis was intrigued. This wasn't the first time that God had spoken into his life. There were so many days that Curtis had given up on himself and felt that no one cared about him anyways. Often in those moments, God would break through in one way or another.

Nathan jumped in with his news: "The message is that I'm supposed to invite you to an Overcomer Conference next weekend here in Ottawa."

"Overcomer? What's that?" Curtis responded. He had never heard of it.

"I went to it last year." explained Nathan. "It's geared towards First Nations people to help them overcome the traumas of their lives, to become free from bondages and addictions or whatever holds them back in life."

Curtis thought about it for a moment. "I'm not First Nations."

Nathan explained, "It's not just for First Nations people. Do you have any baggage from the past, addictions or areas in your life where you feel stuck?"

"Oh yes, of course. Lots of that. But I don't like conferences and I have no money."

"Well, it's not my idea." said Nathan. "Are you telling God you're not interested? All you have to do is come and listen. There will be good music, meals and some people to talk with. I have one free ticket to give away. It's just Friday evening and Saturday all day."

Free food. No reading or writing. Just listening and no small group stuff. There would be worship music. Counselling was optional. And God wanted him to go? Why not?

"Okay." Curtis responded hesitantly as he slipped his tuque back on.

"Cool," said Nathan and he gave Curtis the address and time.

The conference centre was two blocks from the Catholic church so Curtis knew where to find it. The men cleaned up their wrappers and headed out. Nathan gave Curtis a friendly slap on the shoulder. "See you then. I'll wait for you inside the front doors of Ottawa Conference Centre to give you your ticket."

"Okay." Curtis headed home. He didn't really think much about it. Another conference was no big deal to him, yet God wanted him there. Maybe, just maybe, he was a little excited and hopeful.

Chapter 8

Friday night came after the usual weekly routine of TV shows, visiting The Mission for lunch, The Salvation Army for supper and hanging out with his brother and his girlfriend at their apartment. Curtis decided he would go to the conference although he didn't feel that interested.

The smell of coffee wafted out the doors as he approached the conference centre. Upon opening the door, he spied the donuts and made a beeline for them. Things were looking good so far.

As Curtis slipped into the crowd he felt those old familiar feelings of insecurity as people often reacted to his appearance. With his toque and hooded sweater covering his tattoos, he hoped to not attract much attention. He was a studier of people himself, always aware of potential threats or danger. This was why he didn't enjoy being in crowds, especially when he didn't know anyone.

Someone tapped him on the shoulder just after he had picked up his coffee and donut. Curtis swung around, expecting trouble but it was Nathan with his ticket. Curtis took a deep breath and tried to relax.

"Thanks," responded Curtis.

"You can sit with me at the back if you want to, but I will be leaving for a bit during the evening."

Curtis nodded and followed Nathan. The place was quite full. Curtis estimated about four hundred people, the majority who were native. People were chatting quietly as some music played in the background.

Curtis checked his watch. It was 7 p.m. At that precise moment, the Overcomer Band stepped onto stage and started the evening with several songs. Curtis was happy to realize that these songs were familiar from his church in Lavender, British Columbia.

A man named Duane Charlie welcomed them to the conference and gave an outline for the evening and Saturday. This evening two people would share their stories. Saturday would include three main sessions with more singing and stories. There would be workshops in the morning and afternoon. Time slots were available if people wanted to speak to a counsellor.

Before Curtis could evaluate the schedule, a small native woman came to the mike. Curtis guessed she was about fifty-five years old. Duane introduced her briefly and then Lorelle launched into her story.

She was one of eight children, second from last. She said that her parents had been great parents from what she remembered except when her dad was drunk and was beating up her mom. Both parents had grown up with relatives because their parents were unable to care for them.

Of Lorelle's seven siblings, only three were still alive: Joe who was the chief in her home reservation, Ben who held down a good job and had a family, and Luke who had a drinking problem which was taking over his life. She talked about the tragic deaths of the various siblings, about her father who had drowned, and about her mom who had died of cancer at age fifty-two. The deaths of four siblings had come from illness, suicide and drug overdose. All her older siblings had been to residential school, as had her parents. She herself had been forced to go to residential schools until she was ten. At this time, residential schools closed down and so she attended public school. This was perhaps even worse for her. Being the only native girl in the class with all whites except for two native boys had not been comfortable at all. She had been ridiculed and excluded.

The feeling of not belonging, not having a voice and being treated as inferior had led Lorelle to withdraw and eventually she developed a drug addiction to escape her reality. In desperation she went through a treatment program and at the end of the program was offered the opportunity of a job.

She loved her job and her stability, but in five years when she was laid off, she felt lost again. Slowly, she drifted back into drugs and ended up living on the streets of Vancouver for seven years.

After going through another program for a year, she attended an Overcomer Conference where she was emotionally healed of her childhood pain. Now finally she felt peace in being herself. Telling her story helped her break the silence that had engulfed her most of her life.

When Lorelle was done, Nathan walked out onto the stage. Curtis was surprised as he hadn't realized that Nathan had left his spot. Curtis was all ears to hear Nathan's story. As Nathan talked, Curtis became engrossed in his story, realizing that it sounded close to his own: absent father, abusive and neglectful mother, drinking, drugs, no food, messy house and police at the house weekly. There had been no safety or stability. Fear and survival had been Nathan's reality. Curtis had felt this too in his life. He felt himself drifting to his own story of wandering on the streets at age eleven, looking for a place to belong.

Curtis pulled himself back to Nathan's story. He really wanted to know how Nathan's life had turned out. Nathan described himself as a teen: angry, defiant and confused. He had got into drugs and crime until landing in jail got him thinking.

Through this difficult time, he had met a mentor who visited him named Ron. While Nathan spit out his anger and hatred for his family and his life, Ron would listen and encourage him to keep talking. After taking hours to hear Nathan's story, Ron began to help Nathan understand that his past had contributed to his bad choices in life. Nathan could not change his past but his choices in the present could create a new future.

Curtis listened, intrigued. A new future? He wanted that too but it always eluded him. His past always haunted him and there was no escape. Even if for a few hours he could forget his family, his mistakes and his prison years, there was always a dream or a person to shove it in his face again.

Nathan continued. Ron had explained that all people have three basic needs which are absolutely necessary for their well-being. The need to be loved, to belong and to have purpose in life are rarely if ever met, so all of us have to take a look at what was missing in our childhood and find healing where needed. Some people have had abuse or neglect that is obvious and glaring. Others' hurts are more hidden and sometimes there was a situation that affected a child because of the way that person perceived it.

When a child's needs are not met, there is pain, which often extends into adulthood and affects their lives. Children often think that there is something wrong with them and that somehow they were the cause of their troubles.

Curtis didn't really relate there. He felt that his family was the cause of all his problems and that it wasn't his fault. His dad had been high up in the Hell's Angels. He drove a motorcycle with his gang. All his friends were tough like him and most of them had spent time in jail.

While Curtis felt some admiration for his dad's toughness, he remembered that he feared him more. The occasional times that his dad came by the house were times of serious verbal and physical fighting between his parents. As Curtis grew older, his hate for his dad intensified. His dad would bring gifts for all his kids but Curtis wasn't interested; he felt that these gifts were meaningless. He wished for a dad that would love him, spend time with him and help him to navigate through life. That had not happened at all.

Curtis's mind came back to the present. Nathan was wrapping up his talk. He was explaining that he was now so grateful to be experiencing freedom, wholeness and joy. Apparently, Nathan had been able to work through his past with Ron's help, forgiving his parents and others who had hurt him and taking responsibility for his part in his mistakes. Curtis could not deny the zest for life that Nathan had, while in contrast Curtis often felt lost, angry and confused. Nathan exited the stage and returned to his seat beside Curtis.

"Great speech," said Curtis.

"Thanks," responded Nathan "Let's talk more later."

The service ended with a song and an invitation to talk to the counsellors who were standing at the front.

Curtis turned to go but Nathan stopped him, "Hey dude. Where are you at? What did you think about what I said?"

Curtis paused for a moment, "It's good for you bud, but I don't think it would work for me. My life is a right-off and I just have to hang in there until it's my time to go."

"No, don't think like that! Everyone has their own story. Hey, why don't you come and meet my counsellor Ron? He's right up at the front! Let's go!"

Nathan playfully slapped his shoulder and Curtis reluctantly followed him to the front.

Ron looked to be a man in his mid seventies, short, with a balding head. Ron looked into Curtis's face and Curtis felt a warmth rush through him. There was such kindness there, causing Curtis's reservations to fall away and hope to stir.

"Hey Ron, this is my new friend Curtis."

"Yes, Curtis. Nathan mentioned you might come tonight. I'm glad you did."

"Well, I don't really see the point, to be honest. No one can help me. I've made too much of a mess with my life. My daughter won't even talk with me. No one wants to be with me. I've tried. I'm glad you can help all those other people but I'm done."

Curtis's frustration was building up again. Why bother trying or hoping for a better life that never comes? He had changed, hoping his daughter would accept him and that they could start a new life together. But nothing was ever good enough.

"Curtis," Ron's voice cut into his thoughts, "there are reasons that you feel the way you do. You may have had a very hard life but your future can be good. You can be free to be the man that God created you to be. Why not tell me your story? I'm sure that I can help."

Standing there, Curtis didn't know how to respond. Why should he open himself up to more failure and pain? He shrugged. "I guess. Okay. Thanks."

They made arrangements to meet the next morning for breakfast before the conference. Curtis loved eggs and bacon and they decided to meet at a small restaurant close to the conference centre.

Chapter 9

Although Curtis felt a bit nervous about where the conversation might go, he met with Ron at 7:30 on Saturday morning as planned. Ron put him at ease immediately with his relaxing personality and had Curtis talking as soon as the breakfast was ordered. With Ron's encouragement, Curtis shared his life story. It all came pouring out of him. When he finally stopped talking and was silent, Ron just sat there, absorbing it.

"Wow. Curtis I'm so sad for you. So sad for that little boy who was not seen, was not loved and was missed. What a tender soft heart you had as a child and you had to protect it and find your way in a very tough world. I can definitely help you.

"What are you wanting in your life now?" Ron asked.

Curtis didn't even want to think about what he wanted. He had no clue. Why even think of it when the present and the future was so bleak? But Ron was looking at him and waiting patiently.

"Um, peace, I'd love some peace. I don't want to wake up every morning and remember the awful thing that I did or remember my face plastered on every telephone pole in the city, as a man that women should fear. I want to love and be loved. I want a family and I want to belong to someone somewhere. I want to feel safe."

"Yes, Curtis," Ron gently responded, "We all want those things and we all need those things. You did not get your most basic needs met as a child: to be loved, to belong and to know your place in the world. Take a look at this list of feelings. On the left side, check off those you felt as a child and on the right side of each word, check off how you feel now."

Curtis looked at the list and quickly checked off most of the feelings words on both sides. He felt them all as a child and he felt them still.

Ron continued, "Now tell me the three strongest emotions that you feel right now."

Curtis looked over the list and responded. "Rage, abandonment and frustration."

"Okay. Thanks. Now let's look at the list of lies and vows. Check off those that are true for you today."

Curtis quickly read the words. Again it sounded just like him. Ron cut into his thoughts. "So, you checked most of those as well. We have named seven lies: I am worthless, I am not important, I am a failure, I am a mistake, I am incompetent, I am powerless, I am hopeless. So do you feel that way about yourself?"

As Curtis nodded, Ron asked him to pick out the lie he felt most drawn to.

"I am powerless," Curtis blurted out.

"Okay, I have one more question for you Curtis. In the list of vows, which one is strongest for you?"

"I must keep my distance," Curtis said quietly.

"Why would you say that?" Ron gently asked.

"Why wouldn't I say that!?" exploded Curtis. "No one wants me. If they find out what I did and who I am, they want nothing to do with me. I can't get close to anyone. Even my own daughter has rejected me!!"

Ron sat quietly for a few moments, pondering. Yes, he could see the rage clearly. He silently prayed. Lord, please give me wisdom here. Guide me to bring this dear man to peace. He also thought of his wife praying for him and trusted that God would help him.

"So Curtis, you feel that you need to keep away from people so they don't find out about your past. How do you feel about yourself?"

"I'm a loser. I'm a no-good ex-prisoner, good for nothing! I'm stupid! My brothers always said I was stupid and they were right!!"

Curtis slammed his cup onto the table and stormed out of the restaurant. Ron left as well and watched Curtis recklessly run across the street and disappear.

"Well, that didn't go so well." Ron muttered to himself as he drove back to the conference. His wife was waiting for him and was eager to hear about the conversation.

Ron was clearly discouraged. "There is a lot of rage in that man. He took off and I wasn't able to bring him to the place I had hoped for."

Rhonda put her hand in his and prayed, "God, you know where Curtis is right now, his confusion, his hurt and anger. Comfort him and set up another time for Ron to be with him. We put this in your hands. Thanks for all the work that was done this morning."

Ron patted her hand thankfully. "You are right my dear. Thanks."

Chapter 10

The conference continued throughout the day. Ron and Rhonda led an afternoon workshop on abuse. In the evening, Ron would be speaking and then the conference would wrap up with some opportunities for counselling. Ron had organized the fifty volunteers who had all completed his training program. Focused on his present responsibilities, Ron hoped that his conversation with Curtis could continue later.

Ron and Nathan both looked for Curtis in the conference crowd during the day but didn't see him. They kept praying as did Rhonda. At the supper line, Nathan spotted Curtis and went to join him. "Hey man, good to see you."

Curtis grunted and continued to pick up his food. Nathan picked up his dinner as well and followed Curtis to a open table.

"So, how did it go with Ron?"

"Oh, he's alright. I just got upset and left. I hate my life."

"Well it's good to see you now. Staying for the session?" asked Nathan.

"I guess," responded Curtis.

"Well, you will hear Ron's life story tonight."

That interested Curtis. *Let's see what difficult past this buddy had. Who was Ron to think that he could help Curtis?* Curtis kept these thoughts to himself. He went out for a quick smoke and rejoined Nathan in the same spot they had shared the previous night.

After the preliminary music and some announcements about book and cd sales, Ron made his way to the podium.

"Why do I love to counsel people? Why do I love to train people to help others? It's because nothing is more important than people. I don't want to retire and pick up shells on a beach. As long as I'm able, I want to go where there are people who want to be healed from their past and who want to help others. This is what I live for.

"My wife Rhonda and I have been doing this type of work for fifty years now. We started a family ministry soon after we were married. Our focus has been Inuit and Native people in northern Ontario, Alaska, and Greenland. We have also spent some time in India, northern British Columbia, Denmark and Sweden. We have the tools to help set people free from the pain in their hearts. God is the one that provides this healing. There is much I could share about that but you will have to enrol in the counselling course!

"Tonight I will share my personal story. My wife and I were leading a new ministry to help other families. We had two daughters by this time. However, there was a problem. I was an angry man. I didn't want to be but I was and I couldn't figure out why. Rhonda would bring this to my attention but I didn't want to look at it at first. I was a good man and a godly man. Why was I angry and was it a big deal?

"Rhonda had her own issues. She was a very nice woman. I wondered if she was too nice. She was so very pleasant that she really had no emotions. She was not sad, happy or angry but simply flat. She didn't talk much and she never shared her feelings.

"Once we were at a weekend retreat and Rhonda was in a small circle of women. They asked her why she was so quiet and why she never shared her feelings. She didn't know and thought that she was born that way. She felt somewhat numb, like she was living in a fog, but she had been like that for as long as she could remember.

"Rhonda just sat there, not knowing how to respond to the women. Then one of the leaders spoke to her, 'Rhonda, tell us, was there ever a time in your life when you think this might have started? Was there an incident that made you not want to share your feelings?'

"My dear Rhonda closed her eyes and was silent, asking God to reveal to her if there was such a time. Then she said softly, 'Maybe when I was three.'

"'What happened?' asked the leader. Rhonda continued, 'I was three and our family was sitting around the table. There were nine children and I was the youngest. My siblings were all around me and I was very small. It was noisy. I wanted someone to pass me the potatoes but no one heard me so I asked again. And then a third time but still no one heard. I said to myself, no one cares for me. There is no point in talking because no one is listening.   Maybe that was the start.'

"Then the women prayed for that memory and my Rhonda was free. She realized that she was not made that way and she began to get her voice back!

Ron continued, "Now let's go back to my issues. When my wife said I was angry, I didn't believe it. I didn't want to see it but soon I realized that I could not deny it. I was edgy and easily irritated. Angry words came out of me and wounded my loved ones before I could stop them. Clearly I needed help. My wife and I attended a conference and I had the opportunity to speak with a counsellor. Fortunately, it didn't take him long to get to the root of the problem. I was angry at my parents."

Ron explained more about his childhood experience and how he was able to come to a place of forgiveness towards his parents. "That was the beginning of my freedom and my victory over anger. I still have to keep seeking more wholeness but that day released me from the bondage of anger and helped me to understand why I was the way I was.

"Over the past fifty years I have been able to work with thousands of people to help them find the same release from the pain in their hearts and to train them to help others. Only God can give us the grace to forgive those who have wounded us and to forgive ourselves. I would love to talk with you after the meeting and there are trained counsellors also available. We invite you to come and speak with a counsellor. Release your burdens and receive freedom to become the person that God created you to be."

Chapter 11

Curtis was listening intently. What did he have to lose? Ron had also struggled with anger. Ron was confident that he could help Curtis and had listened to him. Before Curtis realized what he was doing, he rushed up the aisle to talk with Ron before anyone else could reach him.

Ron greeted him warmly, "I'm so glad that you came back Curtis. I can talk with you now as I know the other people coming to the front will be cared for."

Ron led Curtis to a nearby corner with two chairs.

"What's on your heart?" he asked.

Curtis responded, "Anger and hatred towards others and myself. It controls me and takes over me. It's always with me. I'm afraid of myself and what I might do."

Curtis sank his head into his arms. "No one can help me though. It's too late. I'm a failure!!"

Ron sat quietly with him, praying under his breath for wisdom and understanding.

"Underneath that rage is a very hurt and broken little boy. Picture yourself when you were a little boy. What was happening?" encouraged Ron.

"I was abandoned and scared," Curtis muttered.

"Who helped you?"

"No one."

"How about your parents or grandparents? Where were your siblings, teachers or other adults in your life?"

"They were there but no one was interested in helping me. It was like I was invisible or they wished I hadn't been born," Curtis stated flatly.

Ron paused again, sharing the fragile moment.

"That shouldn't have happened. That little boy did not get what he needed."

Tears began to run down Curtis' cheeks, unstoppable. His body shook with sobs, which were becoming louder and became wails and groans. He fell on the floor and curled up, continuing to cry uncontrollably.

Ron sat beside him on the floor, waiting and praying. Rhonda had joined them by now as well. Slowly Curtis' sobs subsided and he blew his nose with the tissues provided. Slowly he looked up, now aware that Ron and Rhonda were both with him.

"Wow, what a big baby I am," he said with a slight smile, as he pulled himself back onto his chair.

Ron put his hand on Curtis' shoulder.

"This is the start," he said firmly and gently. "You were not given what was needed. You needed to grieve that in a deep way. Now you will be ready to look at the lies you believed. But this is enough for today. Go rest and sleep. Rhonda and I can meet with you tomorrow for breakfast."

Curtis's brain was foggy. "What? You are busy people. Why would you have time for me? Don't you have to leave the city soon?"

"Curtis, this is your time if you want it. You are very important to God and to us too. There is no greater joy for us in life than to see a person released to be their true self. Let us pray for you."

Ron grasped Curtis's hands in his own. "God, we pray that you would protect Curtis in his healing journey. May he sleep sweetly and deeply tonight. Give him hope for all that you have for him in his beautiful future."

Ron and Rhonda both gave him a hug and Curtis walked out into the night. He felt like he was on a high but not a drug high. It felt like he was being held in love and in peace. He had experienced God before but it had been awhile.

Chapter 12

After the session, Curtis stumbled to his apartment and let himself in. He was exhausted. He lay on his bed with his clothes still on. In the stillness, tears returned and streamed down his cheeks. He lay there and allowed his mind to go back to those unpleasant childhood memories. Then he thought about his life on the streets and cried for that young tough-acting eleven year old that he had been, that teenager looking for love, belonging and security. He cried for the young man that had loved, made terrible mistakes, and lost his partner and their daughter. He wept for the man who was alone and abandoned in jail with his family ashamed of him and his father's buddies berating him. His bed shook with sobs for the lonely wasted years, the drugs and the violence.

He hid his face in his pillow and tried to muffle the billowing sorrow coming from his gut. Then eventually he was done and his body calmed again. He felt God's peace and love on him. He got up, had a long hot shower and made a cup of coffee.

It was now 2 a.m. and the world was quiet, the way Curtis liked it. As he sat at his little table and drank his coffee, he thought about some of the good memories he had.

His psychologist and friend Daniel had met him in prison where Daniel had finally been the one to get through Curtis's tough exterior.   Over time, Daniel had won his trust and had proved to be a faithful counsellor and friend both inside of prison and in the outside world. He had taught Curtis to slow down and think before he acted.

Daniel had been like a father to him, the person he had first loved, the one that helped him to feel again. Tears and feelings that had been buried for years were uncovered with Daniel's help. He had taught Curtis how to process his feelings and to understand that men can be tender.

Most important of all, Daniel had introduced Curtis to God. Curtis had even had a vision of Jesus in prison. He saw Jesus' face and he heard Jesus speaking words of life over him: "Don't give up. Look to me. I bring you hope, joy, love and peace."

The presence of God was so strong and he had recognized it as the presence of love for him as he was right then. New sensations of peace and hope had filled his heart.

Tragically, Daniel was in a terrible car accident three years ago and had suffered badly before his death. Curtis had wept over Daniel's death, realizing that he hadn't cried at all after the death of both of his parents. Now he was able to love and experience the pain of loss.

With Daniel no longer in his life, Curtis had floundered badly, eventually slipping into taking drugs again. He had friends that he'd met at the church who supported him through his crisis. and had kept loving him even when he had made some bad mistakes. But they couldn't help him the way Daniel had and he felt his life spiralling out of control once more.

Thinking over his life, Curtis realized that it was a miracle that he was still alive. Could there still be a reason for his life at age forty-eight after all the failure?

In the quietness, he felt God saying yes, there was more to this life than he had yet known. Curtis got into bed and slept soundly until 9 a.m. the next morning.

Chapter 13

Realizing how late he was for his breakfast meeting with Ron and Rhonda, Curtis hurriedly changed and ran out the door. He hopped on his bike and wove recklessly in and out of traffic, zoomed through three red lights and arrived at Tim Horton's right at 9:30. As he was locking up his bike, Ron and Rhonda showed up.

"Good morning Curtis," they chimed in at the same time.

They headed into the coffee shop, ordered their breakfasts and sat down.

"How did you sleep?" Ron asked, and Curtis told him about his night.

"Good, very good, responded Ron. "God is working in your heart. We have this time with you now and then Rhonda and I will be flying out of the city. Nathan has agreed to meet with you to continue the discussion. What do you think about that?"

"That will be okay," Curtis replied.

He felt somewhat subdued since yesterday. Exhausted really, but also lighter.

Rhonda sat with the men, letting them do most of the talking. Ron appreciated her peaceful presence, her support of him and her care for Curtis.

Ron and Curtis talked for about an hour, going over more of Curtis's life, looking at the beliefs he had carried about himself for so long.

"Grieving your past is a huge step," Ron said. "Seeing how you were formed is crucial. It's often helpful to write a letter to the persons that you feel caused you harm or who helped form your wrong beliefs. Usually it's best not to give them the letter but to write it honestly, share it with a friend, and finally to burn it."

Curtis thought about this. "I've done a lot of work already through Narcotics Anonymous. I feel that I've worked out my anger towards my dad and mom. I probably would start with my grandmother, then my ex-girlfriend and my daughter."

"Yes, start with those and see what happens from there," Ron encouraged him.

"Oh, but there is a problem," Curtis said. "I'm not very good at writing. It takes me a very long time."

"No problem," responded Ron. "We can lend you one of our digital voice recorders. You can talk into it and share it with Nathan later. It's probably best to say it alone initially so you can be free to be honest. Ask God to help you to forgive the person, and then you can speak that out towards the end."

Chapter 14

The next day Curtis checked his mail, hoping for a cheque of fifteen hundred dollars that he had been promised by the Ministry of Social Development. He had to pay his two brothers back several hundred dollars and then he would save most of the rest to get a bus ticket to visit friends in British Columbia. He also wanted to stock up on some household supplies and go out for a few nice meals.

He opened his mailbox and pulled out the envelope! Finally, it was here!! His heart raced. Party time!! Why not have a little fun? Pop some sweet pills and take a break from this life.

Curtis ran to his bank and cashed his cheque. He went home and stuffed the money he owed into a teapot. Under the bathroom sink, he hid some more money for later. That left him with five hundred dollars for a good time.

Two days later Curtis was trying to untangle his fogged brain. He had spent two hundred and fifty dollars on drugs and somehow the other two hundred and fifty dollars had gone missing.

Luckily he had paid his brothers back and bought a few groceries and other essentials. Now the drugs were through his system and reality was coming back into focus.

Curtis remembered that he was to meet Nathan at 2 p.m. on Tuesdays and Fridays at their Tim Horton's. Curtis had **missed** the Tuesday meeting, which he just now realized.

What was he doing taking drugs again? Maybe Nathan wouldn't meet with him anymore and Curtis had thrown away another opportunity for a better life. He was tired of trying so hard to steer his life onto the 'right track', yet he knew he couldn't keep taking drugs. It was too dangerous.

Chapter 15

Lindsey woke up sick again in the morning. She had to rush to make it in time to the bathroom to throw up, then get ready for work at nine. She was so tired these days too. After a week of this, she made an appointment to see her doctor. She was definitely wondering if this was the flu or if it could be pregnancy. She didn't want to think about it even though the thoughts were always hovering in the back of her mind.

Somehow Lindsey made it through another week of work. She loved hairdressing: helping to make women to feel beautiful, offering suggestions on new hair styles, chatting with her regular customers, and meeting new women.

Now she finally sat nervously in the doctor's office, trying to keep from biting her finger nails. Her cell phone buzzed that she had a text. It was Alejandro, who let her know that he was able to leave work at the auto repair shop to join her for the appointment.

She was called into the small patient room but before the doctor entered, Alejandro joined her and they waited together.

Doctor Mallory Simpson had been her doctor since Lindsey was a little girl. Her presence was gentle and comforting.

When the test was done and the doctor returned with the results, Alejandro and Lindsey held their breath. Dr. Simpson was smiling, "It's positive!" Alejandro and Lindsey hugged each other as Lindsey felt relief, joy, fear, and curiosity.

About twenty weeks into the pregnancy, something felt wrong. Lindsey could sense it, but didn't want her mind to go there. The baby had been silent in her over twenty-four hours. The movement had stopped and she felt afraid. She summoned the courage to talk with Alejandro as he was running out the door to work. He had to leave but gave her a quick hug. "Don't worry. See the doctor. Talk later."

On the bus to work, she dialled the doctor's office. A cancellation provided a spot right after work at 4:30. She was relieved but apprehensive. Taking action to see if something was wrong felt good but somehow made the possibility of a problem seem more real. Lindsey's bus arrived at her stop and she set her mind for work. Thoughts of her baby would have to wait until later.

The day flew by quickly and soon Lindsey was in the doctor's office. The baby kicked as soon as Dr. Simpson put the doppler on Lindsey's belly to hear the heartbeat. The doctor explained that babies need time to rest and some days they don't feel like moving.

Lindsey sat on the bus the rest of the way home in a grateful daze. What a roller coaster of emotion! First they got the news that they were expecting a child, then they feared losing him or her, and now she was reassured that the baby was okay. Yet who knew the future? Would the rest of her pregnancy be trouble free? What about the birth? What would life with their child be like? This becoming a mom was an interesting life experience so far.

Traveling home on the bus, Lindsey noticed a man stumbling down the sidewalk, obviously on drugs. She felt disgusted as she thought of her parents' experience with drugs. She looked at the man's face as the bus passed him and saw with horror that it was her own father. She felt sick. Her worst fears were justified: her dad was still an addict. She was relieved that Alejandro had encouraged her to cut things off with him.

Getting off at her stop, Lindsey decided to take a short walk through the nearby park. She wanted to process her thoughts. Having a little one growing inside of her somehow forced her to think about her own beginnings. Loser parents: drug addicts! She would be nothing like they were! Her dad was in jail practically her whole life! At least she knew her mom but that really wasn't any better. Lindsey was taken from her mom and put in permanent foster care. She only got to see her again when Lindsey turned ten and only with supervision of a social worker.

What a mess! Lindsey felt longing and hate for both her parents. Mom was now dead so there was no improving that relationship.

Dad: she didn't even want to think about him. How ridiculous she was to think that somehow he would move from British Columbia to be with her and be a changed man, the father she always longed for. He made her sick: drinking with his brother after she had begged him not to! And clearly, he was still out of control from drugs!

Lindsey's mind pushed away thoughts of her birth parents. There was no point in dwelling on them. She and Alejandro were different and would be good parents. She would ask Alejandro if they could get married as soon as possible. Alejandro had a good job and she could go back to hairdressing after a year-long maternity leave. She would be the mother that she never had.

Their home would be safe and welcoming for their little one.

Leaving the park, Lindsey returned to their home. She felt so dreamy. It felt surreal to think that in four months, she would be carrying their baby into their apartment and having full responsibility of the child's care. Alejandro would be a good father. He loved kids.

She had texted him to let him know that their baby was okay and he had responded with a thumbs up. She was excited to see him over dinner and to talk some more about their future together.

The meal was on the table and Alejandro came home on time. He was his warm energetic self. They sat down to have supper together.

"Hey babe. You feeling okay? That was quite a scare for you with the baby."

"Yah, I'm so relieved! The doctor wasn't worried. In a couple of weeks, we can find out if we are having a boy or a girl!"

"Yah, I wonder about that too. It would be great to know, but either would be great." agreed Alejandro.

"So, Alejandro, I was wondering if we could get married soon, hopefully before the baby comes? It would be wonderful to both have the same last name and be a real family." As Lindsey was talking, she realized how much she wanted this. It was great living with Alejandro, but they hadn't talked about their future together, marriage or commitment.

"Woah, girl. I don't know. I'll have to think about this. I mean, living with you is great. I love you. A baby together sounds fun and exciting, but I haven't really thought long-term."

Lindsey didn't know what to think. She had been on the same wavelength herself: not committed to Alejandro and living in the present. Having a baby was changing her thinking. Now she was beginning to want a stable and committed relationship to offer their child.

After a couple of days of pondering, Alejandro agreed to get married. They wanted to keep it simple and so got married by the Justice of the Peace two weeks later. Lindsey was grateful but did feel a pang of disappointment that her wedding day was not more special.

They celebrated with some close friends with a dinner out after the brief ceremony.

Chapter 16

Curtis woke up on Friday morning around eleven. The drugs had worked their way through his body and his mind was becoming clearer. He remembered that he had a meeting with Nathan at 2 p.m. Curtis rushed out to grab a lunch at the Salvation Army and then went to meet Nathan for coffee at Tim Horton's. He didn't know if Nathan would be there since Curtis had missed the Tuesday appointment, but there he was.

"Hey Curtis," Nathan greeted him, "Great to see you. Where have you been?"

Curtis was committed to honesty for the most part. He told Nathan about his recent experience with the extra money and the drugs. Nathan listened with little reaction.

"Well, you are here now. Ready to carry on?"

"I guess," responded Curtis, "but I don't know if I can do this. I don't seem to change for long. My life goes in circles."

Nathan bought two large coffees, a chocolate donut for himself and a fruit explosion muffin for Curtis. They sat down at a small table by the window and continued their conversation.

"You can't do this. No one can do it alone. It took me five years to get stable and I had Ron helping me every step of the way. God is always there to cry out to. When no one else is there, He is, and He loves you more than anyone else can. Read the Word, brother. Soak yourself in the truth. God loves you. He even knows the number of hairs on our heads. He saves your tears in a bottle. He takes care of the birds and you are much more valuable to Him than birds."

Curtis sank his head into his hands. He was tired. Tired of being angry, tired of seeming to go nowhere and tired of life.

"I just want to be done. I want to die. I hate my life."

Nathan let the words sit in the silence for awhile. "I've been there too. I tried to kill myself sixteen times and almost succeeded multiple times, but I'm still here. I'm guessing that God isn't finished with me yet on this earth. Maybe I'm still here to help you and probably you are here to help others. There are lots of desperate people out there."

"Okay," Curtis said. "I guess I'll carry on. Where are we at?"

Nathan responded, "Ron shared with me that you were going to use a **digital recorder** to speak out your feelings to your grandmother, your ex-girlfriend Jill, and your daughter. Did you get around to doing that?"

Curtis replied, "I did my grandmother but I left the recorder at home. I didn't do my ex or Lindsey."

"Can you tell me a bit more about your grandmother and what you said to her on the recording?"

"Grandmother was cruel. She lived with us and she and my mom argued constantly. I think she hated me. What I said to her was "Grandma, why were you so mean? How could you lock me up in my bedroom?! I was a little child. I hated being trapped in there and there was no way out. The window was very small and jammed shut. I hated hearing you argue with my mom. You scared me because you were so big and rough. I wish that you never lived with us!'"

"Wow!" said Nathan. "Now, can you forgive her?"

"How do I do that? Does that mean that the way she acted was okay?"

"No. Not at all. It means first acknowledging that you were hurt and that her actions were wrong. It also means looking at who she was and why she might have been that way. It's likely that her parents treated her in a similar way. Forgiving her means to release your hatred of her and to agree that you will not treat her in the same way. It doesn't mean that you would accept any more abuse."

"Well, she doesn't deserve to be forgiven. No one should ever treat their grandchild the way she treated me!"

Curtis was silent for a few moments. "Grandma, you messed up my life really badly but I guess I will forgive you. I agree to give up my hatred of you."

Curtis sighed. Forgiveness was a lot of work emotionally. Nathan was wondering if he wanted to continue with the process.

"Now do you want to go on to your ex or daughter with me or would you prefer to do that on your own?" questioned Nathan

Curtis thought for a moment, "I guess we can deal with my daughter now but she rejected me and sometimes I feel that I want to hurt her."

"Talk about that," prodded Nathan.

"When her mother took Lindsey away, I went crazy. I couldn't control Jill's choices but I didn't want to lose my daughter. It's what led to my taking way too much cocaine and alcohol and doing the crime that landed me in jail."

"Keep going."

"I crossed the country for Lindsey three times. She asked me to come this time but now she won't speak to me. I can't try to get in contact with her again and get more rejection. I've tried."

"Start at the beginning," Nathan coached.

"My girlfriend Jill and I met at a drug party. We both were wild and had similar childhoods. Our relationship was abusive but we ended up living together.

When Jill found out she was pregnant, we were both really excited and quit taking drugs. As the baby developed, I began to think of my child's life and I hoped that I could make a better life for him/her than I had. Since Jill had a steady job as a waitress with good tips, we decided that after the baby was six months old and Jill went back to work, that I would be a stay-at-home dad.

"The months flew by and Jill gave birth to a girl. The birthing went well. We were ecstatic with our beautiful baby! I began to think about asking Jill to marry me to offer our daughter Lindsey a secure home.

When Jill went back to work I loved being Lindsey's main caregiver. She preferred me to Jill. She giggled a lot and I got to watch her steady development.

"Since I spent most of my time at home, I met a young woman who lived in the apartment across the hall from ours. We talked a lot. Sometimes she would watch Lindsey if I wanted to have a smoke or needed to run a quick errand. Because of my family history and my time on the streets, my morals were very loose. I had gone to a Catholic Church occasionally with my mom and to a Catholic school but I was not connected to God or His values. So I let things go the way they were going and eventually slept with this girl.

"One day Jill came home unexpectedly and discovered what was going on. She was enraged and she locked me out of the apartment. I went to stay at my brother's place and the next day when I came back, Jill and Lindsey were gone and so was all their stuff.

I couldn't believe it!! I called some people and found out she was with a girlfriend in a nearby town. I decided I was going to kill Jill for leaving and taking away my eighteen-month old daughter. I was on my way there when I suddenly stopped, realizing that I didn't want to ruin my daughter's life. My crazy feelings caused me to feel like jumping out of my skin.

I contacted my buddy and picked up some drugs. I knew how to escape but I took way more than my body could handle on a three-day binge. I was having hallucinations and I have no memory of what happened. After about two days I woke up at my brother's place. Paul was shaking me.

"'Curtis wake up! The cops are coming for you."

'"What are you talking about? Why? I was high but I'm here. Nothing happened."

"There's a report that you did an awful thing. Police are looking for suspects. And their tips are leading to you. Now leave!'

"I was stunned. What had I done? Where should I go? My brother pushed me out the door of his apartment. I jumped on my bike and raced to a park where I hid my bike and myself for three days. I hardly slept and lay there wondering what I had done and how my life might change. After the fourth day, I went to my brother's place at night. Paul let me in.

"'Good. The police didn't find you. This is all over the news. Look in the paper.' There it was: the awful thing I had done, the people who it had affected, and a sketch of my face: the prime suspect."

Nathan had been listening intently. Curtis stopped to see his reaction.

"It's ok. Go on."

"I thought about it: where the crime had taken place, the date and the time. Could it be me? I put my face in my hands and felt a weight on my shoulders. Panic and fear overcame me.

I left my brother's place and walked and walked. At seven in the morning, I went to the police station and asked to speak to an officer. I was arrested and later tried, found guilty and locked up. I was twenty-one years old."

Curtis was silent then. Nathan was silent with him. A tear ran down Curtis's cheek.

Nathan dropped Curtis off at his place and the men promised to resume their conversation the next time they met.

Chapter 17

At the men's next time together, Nathan asked Curtis, "Do you want to talk about your years in prison?"

"Sure, why not? I started out in Kingston Pen. I was terrified. I had done a horrible thing that I had no memory of doing and I hated myself and the drugs and alcohol that allowed me to do that awful thing. I hated Jill for leaving with our daughter.

There I was, trapped for at least ten years. My dad had lots of buddies in prison. I had met some of them before and realized they may recognize my last name and figure out who I was. That scared me since I thought they would harass me.

Sometimes I shared a cell and I didn't feel safe. How would I know that this cell buddy wouldn't harm me in the night? I decided that no-one was going to intimidate me. If someone gave me a hint of trouble I would attack him, and word got around to not mess with me. The other inmates knew that I was fearless. I ended up with a lot of time in solitary. It made me crazy to be all alone but I felt more relaxed to be separate from the prison population.

"I spent some time in a prison in Quebec and then was transferred to Kent Institution in British Columbia, where I continued to be violent to survive and keep myself safe. I got out of prison a couple of times but only lasted for a few days and then I was back in again.

"Three psychologists worked with me in prison but they all gave up because I was so angry.

Then Daniel, another psychologist, came and tried. He was gentlc but firm. I could tell that he was not scared of me. He kept talking with me, trying to get me to open up and gradually I grew to trust him.

After years of working with Daniel, he helped me to see that underneath my tough look was a scared man. I was also a hurting man and beneath that was a tender man who could allow himself to feel his feelings, to trust, and finally to love again.

"When I was released from prison, Daniel helped me to adjust to life on the outside. If I ever needed his help, he came as soon as he could. He got me out of many tricky situations. Every Sunday I went to his home for lunch and spent time with his family.

"Daniel also took me to his church and since I had learned to trust him, I was willing to go into this new environment. It was a foreign place to me, but the people were friendly. There were lots of people and they had money, which I thought could be handy. They met in a school gym instead of a fancy church building. I was restless and wandered around the room a lot, talking to a few people and observing the interactions of people, especially families. I would often go outside for a smoke.

There was lots of talk about a personal relationship with God which was different that what I had experienced in the Catholic church as a child.

Best of all was the music which reached down inside of a deep place inside of me and moved me. No one talked during worship time. Most people seemed lost in their own little world with God. I got quiet too and found rest and peace there and a settling of my body and soul. Words of hope washed over me and sometimes I dared to believe them. I felt wrapped up in love and grew to know that this love was a person: God Himself who is the source of Love. I felt calmer, loved and safe. It helped me to forget my life, struggles, loneliness and guilt for a short time.

I got an iPod from a friend and had his kid load it with worship music. I listened to it all the time and often sang along. I loved to listen to the music loud on my television speakers.

"My life was improving but I still thought about my daughter Lindsey a lot. What had happened to her? The worst thing about being in jail all those years was that I had missed Lindsey growing up. Thinking of her had helped me to want to survive. Now I wanted her to know that her dad loved her and was so very sorry for what had happened. What a mess!!

"When I got out of prison, she was the first person I wanted to call. It took me two months to get her phone number. When I called her and told her who I was, she hung up the phone. She was already twenty-two by then. I was devastated but I tried again six months later. She listened to me long enough for me to give her a contact number if she wanted to call me. After four months, she called the number. We had a short chat and she said that she was willing to see me. As I travelled three nights and days by bus to reach her, my emotions were conflicted by confusion, longing, guilt, pain and hope. I didn't know how it would go.

I met Lindsey with her foster parents. They were polite, sitting at a separate table in the coffee shop to give us some privacy. We kept it to fifteen minutes that first day. The second day we did the same thing but she seemed more closed, upset and didn't talk much.

We scheduled another coffee time the third day but she didn't show up. Her foster dad came and talked to me and said she wasn't ready for me yet. I left the coffee shop without a word, went to my buddy's place and got high. Then I went to my brother's place, got into a fight and hitch-hiked back to B.C. where I knew I was emotionally safe. Daniel always knew how to help me deal with my feelings.

"When I was back in British Columbia, I refused to think about my daughter for awhile. It was too painful to talk about her but I still always longed for her and hoped things would get better. We talked on the phone several times over the years.

Then when her mother Jill died in January 2014, Lindsey begged me to come and to be with her. Seven months later, after only a week-end together, she was done with me."

"And now?" Nathan gently interjected.

"Now? Nothing!" Curtis spat out.

"How does that make you feel?" prodded Nathan.

"It makes me crazy. I wanted her all my life. Losing her caused me such guilt. I was worried about her. Thinking about seeing her got me through many hard days.

Then finally she reached out to me and after several months I came to Ottawa. Now she has slammed the door in my face. I'm furious and I'm hurt. My brain is all messed up about her. I just want to forget about her and I'm not taking any more moves."

Nathan sighed. "Thanks for sharing this with me, Curtis. I'm really sad to hear your story."

The men sat in silence for awhile.

Nathan asked Curtis, "Are you ready to forgive her?"

"Never!" Curtis yelled out and slammed the table with his fist. "She has been so disrespectful. I loved her. No one has messed with my heart like her. I hate her."

Nathan realized that the other customers had stopped their conversations. He motioned for Curtis to go outside with him.

"Curtis, maybe we've done enough for today. You were getting kind of loud in there."

Curtis was suddenly subdued. He lit up a cigarette, "Yes, I get like that. My anger comes out of nowhere. Can you give me a ride home, bud? I don't want to talk anymore right now."

Nathan gave Curtis a ride to his building and they agreed to continue their conversation on Tuesday. Curtis had a long hot shower and then lay down for a rest, with his heart still racing.

Chapter 18

The next Friday morning, the men met again but at a different location.

"Do you feel ready to talk to Lindsey and work out your forgiveness toward her? You can pretend that I am Lindsey. What would you say to me? Be honest."

"Okay," Curtis responded. "Lindsey, you are very selfish. You don't care about anyone else but yourself!

"No, wait. I want to start again.

"Lindsey, I have loved you from your beginning. I was always excited to have you and to care for you as a baby. I am so sorry for how I lived and how I ended up in prison, robbing you of having a father. I could not leave or communicate with you. It tore me up to think of you growing up and me not being able to see you.

"You may have felt that I abandoned you. The truth is that I didn't want to leave you for a moment, yet I was separated from you because of my stupid choices.

"I don't blame you for being confused about me or hating me. Yet you are what kept me going in jail. I wanted to see you again, to make up for the years we had missed and to have a chance to be your father. I wanted to know who you are, what you like and don't like and to know your feelings.

"When I got out of jail I didn't call you much. I wanted to but I was afraid that you would reject me. I wanted to get myself fixed up first so that you wouldn't be ashamed of me and so that you might be proud of me. I felt shame when I made mistakes, thinking that you would not accept me.

"When you called about Jill's passing, I was so sad for what could have been and for you in your sadness. I was also relieved and thankful that you had reached out to me. It gave me hope that deep down you did want me, and even needed me. You begged me to come, to be with you, to comfort you and to help you. I couldn't because I wasn't in a good head space. I didn't have the money. but I thought about it a lot.

"Seven months later I came. I was thinking about you every moment on the bus and envisioning how we could finally have a father/daughter relationship. It was awkward to be together but it was also very wonderful.

"Now you have cut me out of your life with no explanation. And you have not changed your heart all these **seven months** that I've been in Ottawa. How could you do this to me? I love you and I want to be with you. It's impossible to let you go but you will not receive me. You are just like all those other women who slam the door in my face, women who are afraid of me before they give me a chance to show who I really am. I'm not just Curtis Stradmore, the man who did that awful thing thirty years ago!"

"Okay, Curtis. Is there anything else you can tell her? How did all this make you feel?"

"The way you treated me makes me feel terrible. I feel that I gave you my heart and you trampled it. I was vulnerable and you crushed me. I love you fiercely but this hurt you have caused fills me with rage. You are not going to change your mind. You are like an ice block and I need to get out of this city before I hurt you."

"Curtis, can you forgive her now?" Nathan coached.

"I don't know if I can yet," muttered Curtis.

"What is that favourite song you were telling me about that you always listen to and sing?"

Curtis sat for a moment and thought about it. The words were,

The Lord is gracious and compassionate
Slow to anger and rich in love
And the Lord is good to all
He has compassion for all that He has made
As far as the east is from the west…
That's how far,
He has removed our transgressions from us

"So, how has God treated you?"

"He has been kind, compassionate and not angry with me. He has forgiven all that I have done wrong."

"Can you do that for your daughter?'

"I'm not God. I can't."

"Forgiveness does not mean that what she did was okay or that it doesn't hurt. It's not denying what happened or is happening. It's releasing her from your hate and your desire for revenge. It's giving her grace and pardon. Most important of all, it's releasing you from your pain, anger, and hurt which can be the worst prison of all."

"I don't know how," responded Curtis.

"Just start and see how it goes," Nathan prodded.

"Lindsey, I am angry with you because you asked me to come and then you rejected me and won't even give me a chance. I find it hard to forgive you but really it's you I must ask forgiveness of for how my life impacted you.

"Now I forgive you for the great hurt I feel at your rejection. I forgive you for being confused about me, for wanting me but then rejecting me. I forgive you for any feelings of shame you have about who I am. I forgive you for being afraid of me and not trusting me. I forgive you for not giving me a chance. I let you go from all my hopes and desires. I am here if and when you are ready to continue our relationship. Have a good life, baby girl. I will be okay. You don't have to take care of me."

Curtis sunk his head in his arms and was silent for about five minutes. Then he got up and walked out of the coffee shop. He sat on a curb with his head on his arms again, tears running down his cheeks. Nathan followed him out and sat beside him, sharing the moment with him in silence.

Nathan put his arm around Curtis' shoulders and prayed, "God, you heard these heartfelt words. Please release Curtis of his great loss and pain. Fill him with your love and acceptance that he is your son that you have forgiven. You see his heart. You understand his feelings and his true self. Release him from all that holds him back. May Curtis continue to forgive. We give Lindsey to you and ask that you would heal her in all her broken places."

"Curtis, you will probably have to forgive Lindsey again as things come to mind but this is very important work. Let's end here for now and I'll see you next Friday."

Curtis rose and the men hugged.

"Thanks bud. Thanks a lot."

"My pleasure. See you Friday. Go with God."

Curtis felt exhausted after he left Nathan but he also felt lighter and more peaceful. He went home and crashed on his bed.

Chapter 19

The next morning Curtis woke up with a huge weight lifted off of his soul. Instead of dread, he felt somewhat excited and hopeful. With the forgiveness of his daughter behind him, he felt more free. He realized that he had lots of work still to do with forgiveness of others and himself, but a deep release had happened in his soul.

Curtis had been making plans to return to Lavender, British Columbia because his relationship with his daughter was going nowhere and he missed his friends. He had enjoyed his times with his brothers but felt restless to go back to his 'home' and settle in there. He talked this over with Nathan on Friday morning.

"So I've felt worked up for a long time. In the past, when my life got too frustrating, I took drugs to escape. I don't want to do that anymore. I do feel a release from working through my pain and from forgiving my daughter but I'm wondering what to do next.

Should I leave Ontario and return to British Columbia?

"I've also been thinking about my younger sister. She married a prison guard, has had a steady job and children. Of all the five kids in my family, she seems the most stable and successful, yet I've recently heard from my niece that she is not happy. It seems that she is having marriage problems. I've always wanted to have a family of my own and a home. My sister has all that and she has distanced herself from her past, yet she is still not happy. That doesn't make sense to me."

Nathan responded, "I think it's easy for any of us to look at others and think their lives are better, especially when we are struggling. Even if you had all the things that your sister has, there is always someone else who has more. We can reach our goals and still be dissatisfied. There is a hole in each of our hearts that only God can fill. If we can rest in our relationship with Him, everything else is bonus. Peace is much more valuable than money.

Even if you had a wonderful relationship with a woman, life is uncertain and she could become ill, handicapped or pass away. Our only true security is in God. If we can be content with who we are and what we have, that is the best way to live. It's also important to see how we can bless others so life isn't all about us and everyone meeting our wants and expectations."

Curtis continued, "Sometime I feel lost. I don't feel a part of the world I came from. My brother Anthony is not reliable. He seems content to be a drunk and isn't aware of how his girlfriend is using him. He's able to keep his job and that's all he wants. Paul and Joanne are great but they don't really understand me. I feel restless here. I don't want to be around drug addicts and criminals. Yet where do I fit in? I'm not like my friend Troy and never can be."

Nathan mused with him, "We all feel like this at times. We have to start with where we are in life. We can look back on our past, grieve our losses, forgive and let go. We can look at today and realize what we have, appreciate it and use it. We can ask God to show us one thing at a time that we can work on."

Chapter 20

Two weeks later, Curtis boarded the greyhound bus, heading west once more. His long-range plan had been to live in Ottawa with his daughter and siblings but now he was moving away from that dream. He didn't regret the time he spent with his two brothers and his sister-in-law. He felt good knowing that he had done his best to reconnect with Lindsey. She wasn't ready for him yet but he could still hope she would be open in the future. His sister had also closed her heart.

He was a different man than he had been when he got off the bus eight months earlier. Now he was at peace with himself. Even if he found rejection in his own family or in the community, he was thankful for God and for good friends who truly loved him for being Curtis. They didn't look at him with fear because of his past. They saw his heart and hoped for a better future for him.

As he travelled, Curtis's mind wandered to what lay ahead of him in Lavender. The first person he wanted to talk with for a couple of hours was definitely Margaret. He knew that she understood him and cared about him. She had taken leadership of a circle of support for a year when he had needed it the most. She knew important people in the community and was great at talking to them: people like probation officers, cops, members of parliament, support workers and more.

Curtis wasn't so good at talking his way through difficult situations. He was likely to get frustrated and become aggressive, which usually worked against him. He knew he was very lucky to have someone like Margaret on his side. He also wanted her wisdom in his future plans.

Curtis had made arrangements with Troy and Sophie to stay at their place for about ten days. He would unwind and then take steps towards getting settled with housing, finances and a schedule.

He smiled, thinking back to when he first got to know Troy and Sophie. Troy had offered him some part-time work in construction. They had some great talks on the drives into Vancouver and Curtis had enjoyed the work and the money.

When Curtis had been asked to leave his accommodation in a house with several men, Troy had offered him a week at their home. Apparently Sophie was not aware of this decision and reacted strongly. The first night she slept in her teen daughter's room, barricading the door with her body to keep her daughter safe. The second night, she adamantly refused to sleep in the house with Curtis there, asking her two teenagers to come with her to her sister's house. When they insisted they were comfortable to stay home, she asked that they sleep in the same room for night with the door locked. Sophie had slipped out of the house and gone to her sister's house for night. She returned at the next day but was very reserved with Curtis.

The funny part was that now Sophie was a close friend of his and an advocate for him. Even when he made some serious mistakes, she listened to him and believed he could make better choices in the future. She felt that God had given her compassion for him and that God had a good life ahead for him. Sophie's husband Troy was one of few men that Curtis could talk with about almost anything. Curtis respected Troy and wanted to be like him.

Curtis sensed that now it was Troy that was somewhat apprehensive about his return to Lavender. Although he had agreed that Curtis could stay at his home for a short while, Curtis knew that Troy was concerned about the possibility of drugs and about Curtis's potentially negative behaviour in their community. Of course there was plenty of reason for these concerns but Curtis truly hoped that Troy would greet him as a friend and give him a chance once again.

Curtis also looked forward to meeting up again with Ken and Celina and their four children, another family that he had lived with several times. There was also William and Grace, who often had him over for dinner. He was good friends with their son James. There were many others whose names came to mind, people that he had met at church and in the community.

The bus trip was endless and somewhat boring but Curtis passed his time by talking with other passengers and listening to music on his iPod. Finally the bus passed into the Rocky Mountains which were towering and beautiful with snow still on them. Curtis drank in the beauty and was excited when the bus crossed into the province of British Columbia.

The scenery and landmarks were looking more familiar and Curtis's heart began to beat faster in anticipation. It still took about ten hours before the bus pulled into the station in Lavender. Curtis was tired and hungry but more importantly, very relieved and happy to see Margaret, Troy and Sophie waiting for him.

He jumped off the bus and gave them all a big hug. After grabbing his one duffle bag from the luggage area, Curtis talked with his friends and made plans. Troy and Sophie took his belongings to their home and Margaret took him for coffee at Tim Hortons.

Later that afternoon, he arrived at Troy and Sophie's home and was excited to see that their daughter Willow was home as well as their adopted daughter Lucille. He was shown to his temporary room downstairs and settled in while supper was being prepared. After about an hour he was called for supper. It felt great to be back.

Chapter 21

After a few weeks, he found a bachelor basement suite in a home with some people from church. He began to attend two Narcotics Anonymous meetings per week. He was introduced to a man named Dawson who had been through the crime and drug scene after a difficult childhood. Now Dawson was working with recovering addicts in the community. Dawson and Curtis talked and agreed to meet daily for the next month, doing Bible studies together and working through what Curtis wanted help with.

Curtis also went to see his mental health worker once a week and made an appointment with his psychiatrist to evaluate if he needed medication again.

He enjoyed spending time with his friends who were glad to see him again. Going back to church was harder than he had expected. Some people seemed happy to see him, welcomed him back and shook his hand. Others seemed to be avoiding him and he felt like people were talking about him.

Even though Curtis was relieved to be back in Lavender, all the adjustments were stressful. He had stopped his occasional speed and even his pot use before coming back to Lavender, but now he found himself slipping back to smoking pot now and then.

Curtis had to transfer his disability allowance from Ontario to British Columbia and it was taking a long time for this to be processed. He was getting agitated after three weeks had gone by with no money. One day he took the bus to the office to meet with his worker. She had nothing to report and told him he had to keep waiting. She was too busy to spend time with him and he felt the old feelings of impatience and aggression rising up in him. He felt like smashing something. He left the office and slammed the door. Then he briskly walked down the street, hoping not to attract any attention to himself.

Just then his cell phone rang. It was Dawson checking in on him. "Hey Curtis, you were on my mind today. I feel that you might be having a tough time. What's going on?"

This took Curtis's mind off his situation. He explained how he had reacted in the office. Dawson listened patiently. "Let me pray for you."

As Dawson prayed, Curtis' agitation melted away. Dawson reminded him that the Holy Spirit lived in him and that he had the mind of Christ.

"Stay chill, man. Let's meet up for lunch next week and talk more."

Curtis agreed. He felt relieved to have a mentor who was willing to walk him through situations like this. Daniel had always been there before and Curtis sorely missed him. Perhaps God had sent him Dawson for this time of his life as well as the other friends who already supported him. Frustration was usually his immediate response to annoying situations but he realized that his quick reactions often made things worse. Maybe there was a better way. Just maybe, he could change!

The following Tuesday noon, Dawson picked up Curtis and they went through the drive-through at Wendy's Restaurant. Dawson drove to a park and the men ate their lunch in his truck.

"How's your life going, Curtis?" Dawson questioned, "The other day sounded kind of rough."

"Well, your call came just at the right time. I used to blow up all the time, yell and even throw chairs. It gave me a bit of a rush. I'm used to being loud. It makes me feel that I'm in control. Now, I'm coming to realize that it is not the way to solve problems. I'm trying to swallow my anger and calm down before I react."

"I had a lot of anger too," Dawson confessed, "It took me years to learn to control my temper. I lived with a family from age thirteen to eighteen and they taught me how to handle my emotions and how to receive and to give love."

Curtis thought about this. "I've lived with two families from church over several years.

They helped me to see how a normal family lives and how parents love each other and love and teach their children. I wish that I had that growing up."

"Me too," Dawson agreed. "My home was a nightmare. I became a very angry teenager that no one wanted to be around. One day I was looking for a job at a Christian camp but the man I was talking to about the job said that I looked like I needed a family more. I was invited to join his family and he mentored me through many difficult situations. I don't know what would have happened to me if that family wasn't there for me. I'd probably bc in jail or be dead."

Curtis sighed. He hadn't found that type of family when he was young and had spent all those years in prison. There was no point in rehashing that all again. It was time for a new start. He wasn't alone. He had Dawson now and all his other friends to help him. Ultimately, God was the One who was always with him and was his Father, friend and counsellor. Curtis was truly never alone.

Chapter 22

After about five months of living back in Lavender, Curtis's phone rang. It was his daughter Lindsey. His heart leapt but he kept his voice neutral.

"Hi. It's Lindsey. Do you have time to talk?"

"Sure. What's going on?"

"I just found out that you left a few months ago. I wanted to say thanks for coming. It means a lot."

"But you refused to talk with me!"

"I know. I just couldn't do it. My cousin Alexandra told me how well you are doing now. I am happy to hear that. I want to tell you something." Lindsey stopped talking as Curtis waited in silence, wondering what was on her mind.

"I have some news. I had a baby, a baby girl. She's seventeen months old now. I have some extra money and I was wondering if I could come out for a visit and you could meet her."

Curtis was stunned into silence. The phone call was an unexpected surprise and to hear Lindsey say that she wanted to visit him with her baby daughter was incredible news!

"Of course!" he managed to sputter out. "Figure out a time and we'll make it happen."

Curtis paused for a moment and then continued, "Lindsey, can I ask you something?"

When she agreed, he stammered, "Uh, I don't understand. You refused to talk with me when I was in Ottawa. I left the city because I didn't hear from you for months. I didn't think you would ever call me."

"I know," Lindsey said quietly, "Things changed after Emily was born. I began to think how it must have felt for you to lose me. I would die if anything happened to Emily. There is a lot I don't understand but I'm beginning to believe you actually did love me and want me. You didn't plan for your life to turn out the way it did."

Tears rolled down Curtis's cheeks and he couldn't respond. After a few minutes, Lindsey's voice broke into his thoughts as he heard Emily start to wail, "Dad, I have to go but let's give this a try. I'd like you to meet Emily."

A month later, Curtis met Lindsey and his new little granddaughter at the local airport. He felt awkward with Lindsey but Emily smiled at him right away and reached out for him. When he held her for the first time, his heart melted. This little baby was of his blood. Here was a chance to be a grandpa even if they may not see each other often.

Curtis knew that it would be hard to rebuild trust with his daughter, but forgiving her had been a huge release, and now was an opportunity to start over. They got into the nearest airport taxi and headed for the motel where Lindsey and Emily would be staying. Curtis couldn't keep from beaming and he prayed silently to God, thanking him for this delightful blessing.

As the taxi took off, Curtis realized that even more important than a connection with his daughter was having peace with God and knowing that he was living near friends who loved and supported him.

After searching for a place to belong for so long, he was finally home.

Author's Note:

This story is based on a real person's life and most people in the story are real. The true ending of the story is not yet known but this ending is hoped for.

Overcoming trauma and addiction are monumental tasks. When "Curtis" returned from Ottawa, he reunited with his friends but then started taking drugs again. He left for Vancouver, living on the streets for three months. Difficult life-threatening circumstances influenced him to stop all drugs and go to a Christian recovery centre. He was doing well, but after five days he was asked to leave because his physical pain kept him from attending some of the sessions.

Now he is staying with friends temporarily while healing in his body and soul. He is looking forward to working on his goals and finding stable housing. His friends are encouraged by his current choices and look forward to his continued progress.

Comments and questions can be sent to
pain33heart@gmail.com

Song written for 'Curtis'

Could I walk a mile in your shoes
If I could I'd realize just what you've been
through
That has led you to this place
The demons you have faced

Could I walk a mile in your shoes
Do I have the right to presume
That I would choose differently if I had been you
How arrogant and blind
To think I'd get it right
Do I have the right to presume

Tell me your story
If you can trust me
Show me your scars
If you believe I'm listening, really listening

Would it take a miracle of grace
To try to understand each other, whatever it takes
To look you in the eye
To honour what I find
Would it take miracle
Should it take a miracle
Could I walk a mile with you

Could I wear your shoes
What if I were you

Made in the USA
Lexington, KY
06 April 2017